Michael McMahon

Why Do the Stars Shine?

and other questions about the solar system

WHY IS IT SO? Science

CAMBRIDGE UNIVERSITY PRESS

What is the Milky Way?
Why do the stars shine?

Contents

Questions about the stars 4
Questions about the solar system 6
It's a fact 8
Can you believe it? 10
Who found out? 12
It's quiz time! 14
Glossary 16

Questions about the stars

the Milky Way

Q: Why do the stars shine?

A: Stars are balls of hot gas. They are a very long way away, so they look like sparkling points of light. A star begins to shine when it gets very hot in the middle and releases energy, producing heat and light.

Q: What is the galaxy?

A: The galaxy is all the stars we can see in the sky – every **constellation** and all the star clusters we can see through telescopes. There are 200 billion stars in the galaxy.

star clusters

Q: What is the Milky Way?

A: The Milky Way is the name of the galaxy that we live in. We call our galaxy the 'Milky Way' because from Earth it looks like a wide, white road leading into space.

Q: When and where can you see the Milky Way?

A: The best time to see the Milky Way is on a clear winter night. The best place to see it is in the country, far away from bright lights. The closer you are to the **equator**, the more you can see.

More about stars

- Stars are not 'star' shaped.
- Stars are bigger than **planets**.
- Our Sun is a star.
- Stars are born, live for billions of years and then die.
- They change size as they use up their gas.
- A star dies when all the gas inside it is used up.

Questions about the solar system

Q: What is the solar system?

A: The solar system is made up of the Sun together with the eight planets, **comets** and small **asteroids** that **orbit** around it. At the edge of the solar system there are millions of ice balls.

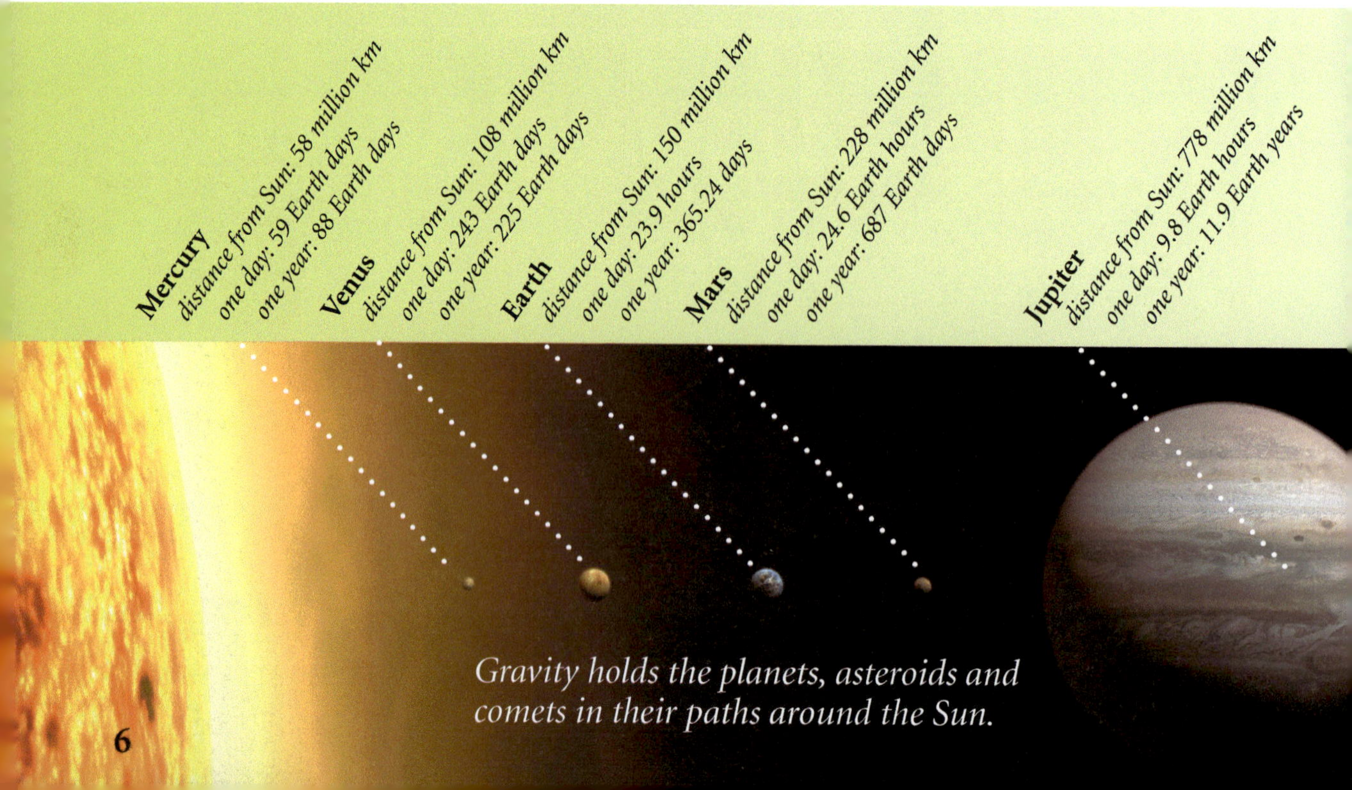

Gravity holds the planets, asteroids and comets in their paths around the Sun.

Q: Where did the Moon come from?

A: The Moon was made millions of years ago. We do not know for sure how it was made, but most scientists think that a small planet crashed into the Earth. The **collision blasted** huge pieces of the Earth's surface into space. These pieces of Earth came together in an orbit around the Earth and became the Moon.

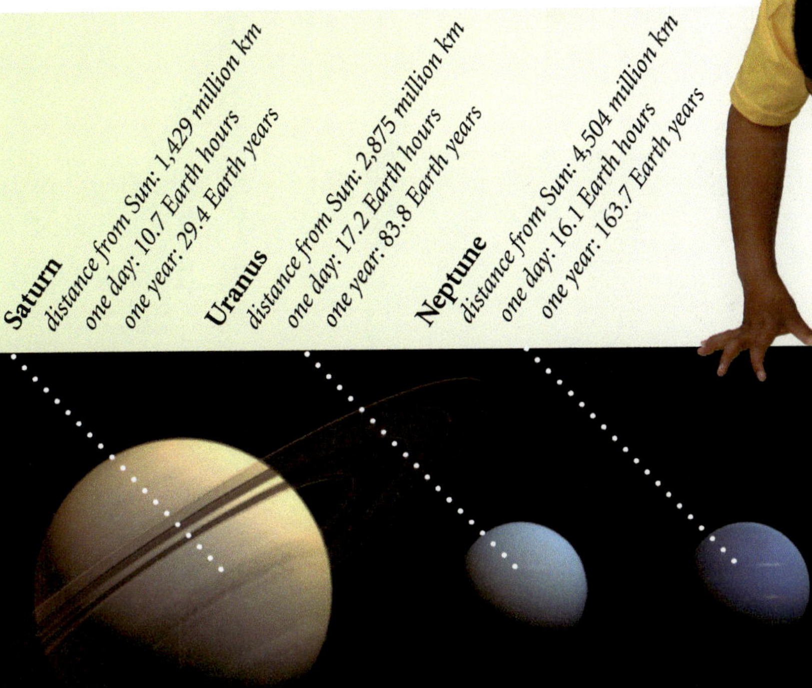

The biggest planet in the solar system is Jupiter. It is so big that all the other planets could fit inside it.

It's a fact

Mars

> Speedway

The Sun, Earth and the rest of the solar system travel around the Milky Way at up to 900,000 kilometres per hour (km/h). Earth goes around the Sun at about 107,000 km/h.

> Moon size

The Moon has the same surface area as the continent of Africa.

> Halley's Comet

Halley's Comet is the most famous comet. It is named after Edmund Halley, who saw the comet in 1758. People last saw it in 1986.

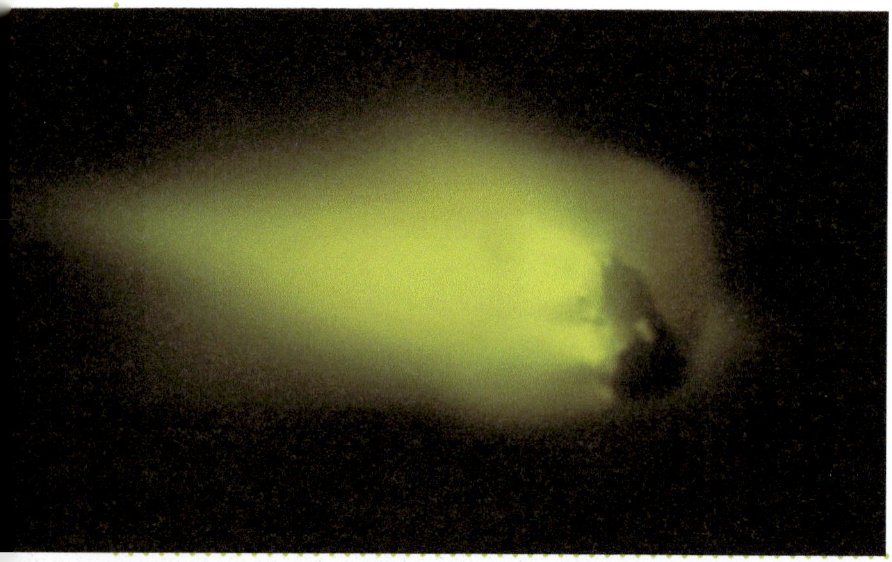

Halley's Comet

> The red planet

Mars is often called 'the red planet' because it looks red. The Romans named the planet Mars after their god of war because red is the colour of blood and fire.

> Supernova

A supernova is a star that destroys itself in a huge explosion. They are very bright and you can see them in the sky in the daytime.

> The names of planets

Most of the planets are named after Roman gods. Venus has the name of the goddess of love and beauty because it is the brightest planet. Mercury has the name of the messenger god because it moves fast across the sky.

a supernova

Can you believe it?

the Moon

the Mars Observer *probe*

Disaster!

The *Mars Observer* cost a billion dollars, but it only took one photo. It blew up in 1993 before it reached Mars.

Comet Halle-Bopp

When Comet Halle-Bopp was near the Sun for a year, it put 8 tonnes of water into space every second.

Time travel

On 21 December 1968 *Apollo 8* travelled to the Moon. It took only three days.

the Apollo spacecraft

a black hole

Black holes

When a huge star collapses, it creates an area of intense gravity – a **black hole**. A black hole eats up everything that comes near it, including light.

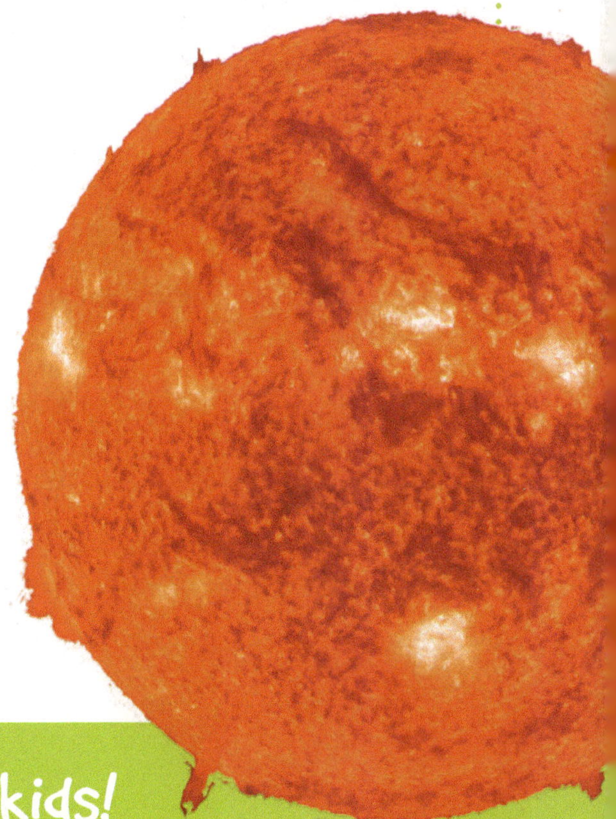

Energy from the Sun

In one second the Sun sends out more energy than people have used in all history.

Always moving

You are moving at about 107,000 kilometres per hour all the time. That's how fast the Earth is travelling around the Sun.

Solar system website for kids!

http://antwrp.gsfc.nasa.gov/apod/astropix.html

Who found out?

Earth's orbit: Nicolaus Copernicus

Nicolaus Copernicus (1473–1543) was a Polish mathematician and **astronomer**. In 1514 he said that the Earth turned on its **axis** and moved around the Sun in one complete year. People did not believe him, but Galileo and other astronomers later helped to show that his idea was correct.

Supernova: Tycho Brahe

Tycho Brahe (1546–1601) was a Danish astronomer. In 1572 he saw a new star that was as bright as Venus. It was the brightest supernova for 500 years. People were very surprised by his discovery because they thought that stars never changed.

Dr Vera Cooper Rubin

Dr Vera Cooper Rubin (1928–) is an American astronomer. She discovered that galaxies are surrounded by clouds of invisible dark matter. Astronomers still do not know what it is.

Carolyn Shoemaker

Carolyn Shoemaker (1929–) is also an American astronomer. She has discovered more planets than anyone else. She has found more than 800 asteroids and 32 comets and co-discovered Comet Shoemaker-Levy 9. In 1992 this comet travelled too near to Jupiter and broke into 21 pieces.

It's quiz time!

1 Choose the correct words.

1. The best time to see the Milky Way is (in the morning / on a summer night / on a clear winter night).
2. The (Sun / Moon / Earth) and everything that circles around it is known as the solar system.
3. Mars is often called the (Yellow / Orange / Red) Planet because of its colour.

2 True (T) or false (F)? Correct the false ones.

1. Stars are balls of hot gas. T

____

2. A supernova is a star that keeps shining. ___

____

3. All the stars you see in the sky belong to our galaxy. ___

____

4. Planets are bigger than stars. ___

____

5. Stars are born, live for billions of years and then die. ___

____

3 Solve the crossword.

Across

3. The Sun is a ________ .
4. 23.9 hours make one Earth ________ .
5. The brightest planet is ________ .
6. Stars are balls of hot ________ .
7. A star releases ________ , producing heat and light.

Down

1. The sixth planet from the Sun is ________ .
2. All the stars you can see are in our ________ .

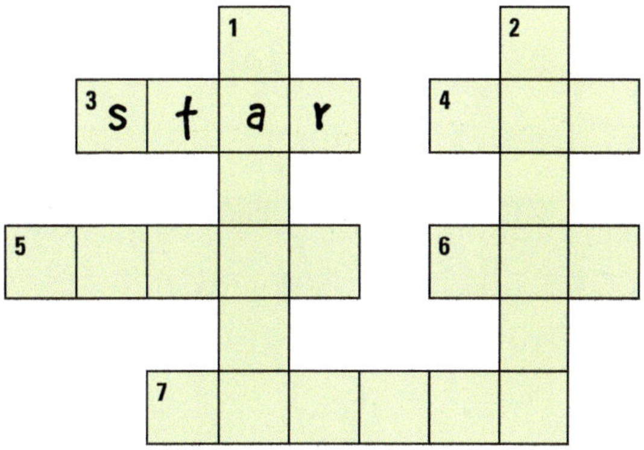

4 Rewrite the sentence with gaps between the words.

ThesolarsystemismadeupoftheSuntogetherwiththeeightplanets cometsandsmallasteroidsthatorbitaroundit.

____

____

Glossary

asteroids: small, planetary bodies

astronomer: a scientist who studies stars, planets and space

axis: the line around which a rotating body turns

black hole: a region in space with extremely strong gravity that eats up everything that comes near

blast: explode and throw things out in many directions

collision: two moving objects hit one another violently

comets: objects moving across the sky with bright tails of light

constellation: any pattern into which stars are grouped and named

equator: a line around the middle of the Earth, an equal distance between the North Pole and the South Pole

orbit: to move in a curved path around a planet or other body in space

planets: large round masses of rock and metal (for example, Earth), or of gas (for example, Jupiter), which move around a star